ABOUT THE AUTHOR

Elizabeth McGeown is a Pushcart Prize-nominated writer and performer from Belfast, Northern Ireland. She is the 2022 UK Slam Champion, a three-time All-Ulster (Northern Irish) Slam Champion and has twice been longlisted for Best Spoken Word Performer in the Saboteur Awards. Her work has appeared or is forthcoming in *Banshee*, *Abridged* and *Under the Radar* and she is currently studying an MA in Creative Writing (part-time) at the University of Birmingham. She was funded by the Arts Council of Northern Ireland and University of Atypical to write her first full-length spoken word show *Cockroach*.

Website: https://elizabethmcgeown.com/
Instagram: candys_eyes
Twitter: @CandysEyes

Elizabeth McGeown
COCKROACH

PUBLISHED BY VERVE POETRY PRESS
https://vervepoetrypress.com
mail@vervepoetrypress.com

All rights reserved
© 2022 Elizabeth McGeown
The right of Elizabeth McGeown to be identified as author of this work has been asserted in accordance with section 77 of the Copyright, Designs and Patents Act 1988.

No part of this work may be reproduced, stored or transmitted in any form or by any means, graphic, electronic, recorded or mechanical, without the prior written permission of the publisher.

FIRST PUBLISHED JULY 2022

Printed and bound in the UK
by ImprintDigital, Exeter

ISBN: 978-1-913917-12-8

Cover artist: Joni Marie Augustine
Instagram: https://www.instagram.com/j0ni_augustine/

To my Mum, who raised a punk (my sister) and a goth (me) and still thinks she is boring. She isn't.

If you are a person who retweets that Kim Addonizio poem every time it comes up in your timeline, this book is for you.

CONTENTS

Origin Story

Cuckoo	12
Ritual for the Creation of a Tiny Goddess	13
Villain (i)	14
The Curse	15
Witch	19
Column	26
Classic Movie Night	28
Villain (ii)	29

The World Beyond The Tower

ieCarrieCarrieCarrieCarrieCarrieCarrieCa	32
Simon Said	33
How to Self-administer an Enema	36
Villain (iii)	38
Gatekeeper	39
Villain (iv)	43
Enema Redux	44
Villain (v)	46
The Beast Approaches: A Tragedy In Ten House Parties	47
Intermission/Larvae	51
Dreamboy	52

The Rape of Solitaire	54
Villain (vi)	58
The Hose, Again	59
Villain (vii)	60
Cockroach	61
Villain (viii)	64
Slug	65
Villain (ix)	67
When is a Body not a Body?	68
Snake, Seductive	69

Becoming

Butterfly	72
Villain (x)	73
Today, I thought of Eyam	74
Villain (xi)	82
Blood/Dogs	83
Three Fictional Women Meme	88
Villain (xii)	92
Swan/Suddenly/Suzanne	93
Villain (xiii)	97
The Writing Workshop as Place of Misunderstanding	98
Misophonia	100
To Elizabeth, Crying Uncontrollably in the Next Stall	105
Three Fictional Women Meme (ii)	107

Villain (xiv)	108
In an attempt to try and redirect your unhealthy lockdown parasocial obsession with the poet	109
Villain (xv)	111
My Clinic	112
Villain (xvi)	115

Notes & Acknowledgements

COCKROACH

Origin Story

Cuckoo

Children stare at me
They are blonde, so blonde! You must
think of a brick wall.

Ritual for the Creation of a Tiny Goddess

They have no blindfold. Instead, they form
a queerly solemn procession: one, guided
by another holding her hand, speaking softly
to her in a quiet voice; the third — the tallest
— for practical reasons walks behind, hands over
the eyes of the chosen one. Gentle
instructions are whispered. Girl is manipulated
and turned. Guide opens a gate which makes
a squeaky hinge sound and this is not correct
procedure. Girl rears up like a nervous colt:
there's a jolt in the cortege, the human blind-
fold collides with her back. A gate means a garden
and someone else's garden is not part of the game,
Girl knows. Girl has played this game before.

Girl is reassured soothingly, hair stroked,
spoken to in horse-whispering voices. Girl stills.
Guide asks her to reach out a hand, takes it
as if to place it somewhere and this, again, is not
correct   procedure.
There is no good reason for her hand to be placed
anywhere by anyone else inside a metal gate's
boundaries. Someone else's property. Girl stops
completely, spell broken, claws hands from eyes
to look upon a bristling patch of Stinging Nettles,
yearning for her touch. Laughter   breaks!
Girl is all at once horrified, and not surprised at all.

Somewhere, plates are shifting. A pattern is being set.

Villain (i)

In which The Cockroach searches for her face in the wonderful world of The Movies!

In childhood   a recurring dream.
I would battle Superman, trying to defeat him
but he won with
his greater strength,
his greater truth,
justice and the American way.

I was defeated and would sit,
feeling the hope seep out of me,
so powerless against these good people,
these firm-jawed, straight-teeth people,
these 'heroes'.
I would make a fist — at six, *a fist!* —
knowing it was nothing
compared to Hollywood gloss.

Why did I see myself as the villain?

The Curse

In which The Parents wonder where The Cockroach came from

When you begin to wonder if your child is cursed,
something has gone fearfully wrong.

THE PARENTS SPEAK OVER EACH OTHER IN
A CACOPHONY! —
When you tell her,
you have either given up   all hope or
are in the middle   of some respite
suspecting it was   not the case,
things are going well now,   let us speak of the time
we thought you were   the cursed daughter,
could not talk   to others,
did not know why   (and nor did I).
Let us laugh at how crazy, ha!   How paranoid!
Look at you, you thrive!   It has not always been so.

When she was small
she would memorise
and win prizes, recite parrot-fashion
and they gave her applause
and book tokens. This girl!
This girl has book tokens coming out of her ears!
This girl has Sunday School certificates!
This girl is a fruit machine. Pull the lever
of this one-armed bandit
and she will ker-ching-ching-ching,
bounty will rattle metallically out of her.

FRED SAVAGE NARRATES FOR THE FATHER:
You probably wanted a son though.
Wouldn't an athlete be so much easier?
He can run and jump and eat and sleep.
Buddies! You can be buddies!
You can be sporting buddies.
You have tried to reach out
to her in so many ways.
The Father-daughter swimming trips
she doesn't seem to take seriously
preferring to splash, and bob, and play.
The sports day training sessions
with a series of obstacles: beams across
the path and she will jump
and this will be her road to athleticism.
You do not understand why she cries;
trips over a beam and just lies there.
She told you she was not good at sport
so she must have wanted to improve.
Correct? It must be. No-one is content
with substandard physical effort.
You just wish she would stop crying.
It stands to reason that total immersion
will help. Wear the roller skates indoors
for several hours a day until you are skilful.
Why would she stage a sit-down protest?
Everyone wants to fly.

The father-daughter cycle days
when you speed up to see
if she can catch up with you.
You stop
and five minutes later
she   ambles   round the corner

puffing-pushing-pedals
not realising you were timing her.
You didn't tell her it was a race,
assuming she would be aware
of the competition
inherent in every life situation.

Your daughter stopped to smell the flowers.

You find yourself measuring
her strength/speed/agility against
the other street-children in the estate
and she is coming up wanting.

> SALLY FIELD NARRATES FOR THE MOTHER:
> Anything for a quiet life.
> You really just would do anything for a quiet life.
> Unfortunately you married into noise
> and spend most days soothing
> his moods, your poor ears.
> You really think the child is fine.
> Look! She derives pleasure
> from books, from television,
> from close female friendships
> with the other street-children in the estate.
> You just wish those friendships weren't so rocky.
> They change their minds
> with so much speed your head spins
> and if your head spins, hers aches
> with the strategies she must learn.
> She must be a weathervane,
> unresisting to whichever way the wind blows.
> Not hold grudges when they blow the other way.
> You tell her that she will not always be wanted

so, at times, must be grateful for scraps.
Look for:
new kids in the district,
summer schemes,
the others who lack popularity
and bring laughter down upon themselves.
These will be your allies, child.
Do not look down on them;
you are one of them. And this works!
(a misfit + a misfit = a kind of sanctuary)
Someone who will never laugh at you
until one by one
the misfits move out of the estate.
Upwardly mobile parents
and she tries to cling on but
before mass internet it is a losing battle.
Everyone disappears
and you wonder, again,
if your child is cursed.

Witch

In which The Cockroach attempts institutional learning

I.

Witch!
I was witch because my hair
would not do what it should:
invading personal space,
schoolbooks and sticking to walls;
because I spellcasted with my hands
in fingerlong motions; because I would sing
without giggling first as an apologetic
precursor to drawing attention to myself;
because I did not pay the daily toll
and call Angela pretty
when the prettiest thing about her was
the relief we felt when she left.

Recognised, I warned them
to be careful, as witches can punish.
My friend pursed nervous lips
You shouldn't have said that.

I think it was exactly what I should have said.

But they can punish too and in the worst way.
I was demoted. No longer feral,
strangely respected and feared,
my importance was erased.
Jeers of *boooor-ing!*
so loud and so long that

I graduated vocally scarred.
Never being allowed to finish a —
Having to relearn how to speak.

I was too young and not yet
in my powers. Bleeding was irregular
and new. I whispered
chants wrongly, mispronounced
the ancient tomes and they knew
I could not defend myself,
increased in brutal wickedness.

I sat in a bathtub and watched
the signs of puberty sneak up
on me. It seemed I had always
been smoothing leg hairs flat
with bathwater. Unaware of shaving,
they whispered it at me, followed me with hisses
and I shaved, once, for their grasping inspection.
Thick, dark tights ever after as I realised
I should not reveal my true nature.
If they wondered, let them wonder.
I would never again show sacredness
to those who would make me change it.

You died many times,
you all died many times.
Remember the twinges?
The headaches in Geography?
It hurt me as much as it hurt you,
I bored into the back of your neck;
pinhole voodoo surgery
rearranging blood vessels.
Nosebleeds in English Lit

led to searing cauterisations.
Black Cat yawns, white
fangs displaaaaaaaayed.

But seven times seven times seven
comes back against you.
Cat died and somehow they found out.
Pinned to the wall with laughter, jeers,
scissors... or not so open. Behind back
they crept, they cut
a hank of hair
to throw back in my face.
I, Samsoned was broken;
the only time I ever truly wept.

II.

I would stitch the shining scales of the lizard
together to make a Chameleon cloak.
What colour am I now?
I am navy blue, your colour, one of you!
My voice higher pitched than theirs
or more resonant;
something that set off their alarms,
the glamour not staying quite in place.

I had to flit
between groups lest I be
                                      uncovered.
My shoulders began to turn inward.

I made a deal with the devil,
which is to say,
being unsure of his existence,

that I made a deal with myself;
I would survive this.

From baby, we are encouraged to up, up!
Prams, cots, beds, shoes
protect cold feet from the ground.
Look at the sky, the stars!
Bathe in it,
          don't look down,
hand sanitiser for daring to touch the Earth
but a series of dreams occurred,
telling me to plunge my hands in soil,
caress tree roots.

 Why do we reject grounding?

Feel the dry chunks of mud between your fingers,
as far up as wrists sometimes, as far as you need to go.
Terraced house sends you to forest, to park.
Dirty hands pay the bus driver,
who raises a single eyebrow.
You will survive this.

You circle yourself in salt;
you circle of salt yourself.
We are an island surrounded by
a wide blue circle of salt every day.
We swim in it.
It should protect us:
salt sea circle survivors.
It does not. We are unsafe.
I will survive this.

Drink my tears
and taste my blood
and watch and wait,
swirling spittle round a
you-must-be-quiet! mouth.

III.

I died many times too
and it gets boring. *Boooooringgggg!*
As the ducking mechanism rises
eyes fill with water,
water
        falls
                away.
Water rises in my lungs and I become numb.
Days passed and water would not destroy me:
Water whispered comfort to me.

Pulled from the stool — muscles cramped
and aching from the long sit —
to the pyre.

I awoke underneath cold embers,
long having ceased to smoulder.

I, brittle and thin,
gathered up my charred sticks of bones.
Fingerlong skinless hands
lifted a dessicated heart from the ash.

        I would survive this.

I ran to the woods, fitted
heart inside my chest.
Here, I was in agonies
as skin grew back
in easily torn layers
softly wrapped in sphagnum.

Here I learned;
Friend Tree sheltered me
as I learned how to speak to the birds:
first rasping clicks,
later, something akin to music.
I practiced walking
on rust-coloured smoke-stained femurs,
pelvis shuddering.
It took years. Is still taking years.

IV.

Flash forward to now!
See me use modern phrases?
See my almost-eye contact.
See me converse casually
and shop for foodstuffs using either
cashier   or   self-service machine
with equal ease!
I can juggle your punchlines and hit a home run,
I can have a human kind of fun.

But I will always flinch,
I will always leave too quick
(before you tire of me),
I will always know you are lying
and when I go, hurt and healing,

surviving in the shadows,
you will always think you detect
an almost imperceptible smell of burning.

Column

In which The Cockroach tries to stand straight in a curved shell!

The man told me of a string
coming from the sky
attached to the top of your head —
elongate your spine and think about this string!
I was never convinced.
Where does it enter the skull?
I never found a motivating metaphor
until ballet told me to imagine
a meat hook through my chest, heaving me up;
movie corpse hefted by butcher
perhaps not quite dead
yet breathing tight around the metal.
Which is worse, the pierce
or the cold steel curve for leverage?
The pull, is it hard yank or slow drag?
A dentist removing a tooth comes to mind,
when they bear down and wrench it out
breastbone involuntarily rises upwards.
Head may do what head does,
head lolls but chest is
proud suit of armour walking by itself.

The man (the physiotherapist) told me
those with Fibromyalgia or
Myalgic Encephalomyelitis or
Or/Or/Or
have more postural problems
because of the extra effort
breathes

it takes
breathes
to stand straight.
End of day a gradually deflating doll,
slumped,
hunched,
spine not a snake,
    not a
        slithering,
            sinuous
        intuitive
          entity
        but a discrete set of instructions
that must be read singly.

Erecting a tent while the canvas
collapses comically around you;
scrabbling for the next piece of Lego.
(*No, the red one*
Where's –
No, red!)
Shifting Tetris blocks
in a four-tier sequence of movements.

I gradually lurch forward:
a curving arc.
This is my birthright.

Classic Movie Night

In which The Cockroach immerses herself in cult classics, assuming she is Rowan and finds she is instead The Fool

He investigates
the disappearance of young
Rowan Morrison.

Hand of Glory waits.
These people lie, are tricksters.
Circle ever tightens.

(there are no bees here.
You're thinking of the wrong one.
Not one single bee)

A man who is a
fool. Who comes here as virgin,
of his own free will.

You are burning slow.
Surrounded by birds and beasts;
Pagan offering.

Rowan never lost;
smiles with family, you scream
'Oh, Jesus Christ, No!'

Villain (ii)

*A video circulates on the internet.
An autistic blind girl plays guitar for the first time
and we are meant to be moved
by her reaction to the music.
Prior to reaching out and touching
the guitar she shakes
her hands repeatedly.
The internet tells me this is a stim:
repeated movements or sounds
that stimulate one's own senses,
most prevalent in people with
Autism Spectrum Disorders.*

The World Beyond The Tower

ieCarrieCarrieCarrieCarrieCarrieCarrieCa

Hear your Mother's voice:
'They're all gonna laugh at you!'
Burn the city down.

Simon Said

In which The Cockroach attempts to lift her voice to sing

We are the incredible shrinking women.
Faces hidden behind hair,
bashfully gazing at our feet
in the cracks between the fat cheeks
of the men who do not say as much,
do as much, who do nothing
but drink together, play together,
stay together, say together
all their words on bills, on posters,
on line ups of the best, the greatest
the *Let's give him the gig
because Johnny's my mate-est.*

I used to be
in the music industry
in a way, in a manner of speaking,
peeking my head above the parapet
not quite yet being able to touch success;
the other bands being out of hand's reach.
Although I could probably touch if I asked nicely:
blowjobs for the boys are always popular.
I would have been allowed
to be in their crowd. So proud!
I never experienced overt sexism.
No *Get your tits out!* shout
They were blind to me.
My cloak of invisibility.
Eyes slid off me, the human banana skin
in a singer's clothing.

You forget though. And it's been years
since I sang, since empty bar rooms rang
with my voice, since the testing... *one two,
one two* and who do you think you are anyway
to grandstand in this man's land?
Singers ten a penny and they snigger,
pass a cigarette around and titter.
He's the phantom in this opera,
you're the angel of music.
Take direction, pass inspection.
Present my careful lyrics for inspection.
Edited and edited
but very rarely credited as mine.
She sings great, looks great, mate but can't create.
But can't ever create.
Simon said *You can help with songwriting*
and yet... and yet.
My head above the parapet,
peeking. Eyes open/eyes closed.
Simon said he must see if my lyrics
are good enough first.
I asked who okayed his.

I, who had been creating
for most of my life could not
understand what was happening.
That girls just do the sing thing
but cannot have awakenings
or labourings or figurings or renderings.
They must just do the listening
and they should count their blessings
in spite of their misgivings.
They're trying to make a living
in the wrong place.

And yet, my head above the parapet.
Glass ceiling reeling from the impact,
skull cracked, neck back, whiplash
crash back down to the floor.
You won't peek over anymore, will you?
And so you don't.

How to Correctly Self-Administer an Enema

In which The Cockroach follows her gut

Lubricate the tip.
You have been instructed to do this twice a day,
this gets wearing
so it helps if you
lubricate the tip
              before insertion.

You will get so familiar with the curve
          of your belly, your buttocks,
              you will lie with them
                  uncovered
                twice a day
             so it helps if you
           get used to them.

Change the angle of your knees for experimentation:
the instruction booklet tells you
                  you might like to try
placing one foot flat on the bed
                  when you lie on your side, top leg
crooked above a straight lower leg
            preparing the angle of entry.

This might not work for everyone
so you can try hugging your knees to you,
your belly compacted.

The solid barrel of it increases
the long line of hips/buttocks/thighs
which you stroke in a continuous
feather-light movement.

You are a painting.

Villain (iii)

I searched for my face as a child.
And the faces I found were not
                  High School Musical
                  Saved by the Bell.
The faces I found
were more often than not:
                  Jack Nicholson.

Jack, panting, slack-jawed drooling bull
in The Shining as the Overlook Hotel
drains his humanity
animation from his face,
leaving him bovine and axe-carrying,
only breathing, only all mouth.
I felt that slackness in my own face at end of day
I could switch off,
animation off,
human off
need to please society off
simply let jaw hang,
gulping oxygen and resting muscles:
emotional as well as physical.

Gatekeeper

In which The Cockroach comes up against barriers and borders and Brexits

Gatekeeper you are / the Gatekeeper / are you *my* Gatekeeper? You are straight / white male / have always been straight / white male / will always be straight white male / will never be more complex / you speak of canon / William Shakespeare wrote plays / or / Francis Bacon wrote plays / or Christpher Marlowe wrote plays / it is as it should be / one straight one straight white male / fighting / another straight white male / for supremacy and ownership / authorship / ~~don't look too closely at Marlowe's / Bacon's personal life~~ / doesn't matter who wrote it really / it is canon / it is as it should be / the gate is kept / The Bible was written / by God / and we are in His image / but some are more / in His image than others / and / straight white male / begat straight white male / MatthewMarkLukeJohn / where are all the people of that land? The gate is kept.

Gatekeeper you are changing / female / you are becoming female / gate clangs shut / you pant, breathless / in by skin / of teeth / wrap small / determined fists around metal posts / symbolically pluck / a lengthy hair from your head / tie it closed behind you / one / survival of the fittest / one is you / but no / more / no more / two is careless / two is floodgates / Gatekeeper will have no floodgates / casually slice / red pen through Sadie's work / Sadie sits in class / and daydreams / must try harder.

Gatekeeper / in Ireland it is not / simple / a choice between male and female / we laugh / *together* here / a single focal point / the pinnacle / of laughter / craic / Guinness! / storytellers converge / in Dublin / University town / magnetised by the house of learning / all the craic / pat each other on the back / Dublin you are / the Gate / if you were serious / you would move here

Belfast no man's land / accent harsh / to refined ears / Dublin / doesn't get why you take yourself so seriously / Dublin thinks you should / enjoy while they display / their privilege for you / their newest names / come / and sit in audiences / admire from afar / feel free to visit / open Gate to audiences / always need a paying / audience

If the British / wanted us so much / they could make room / surely? / they clung on / for hundreds of years / dragging us / kicking and screaming / their Brexit beneficiaries / *Brits out!* / forgiven / just listen to us / listen to our stories / listen to our histories / listen to our Bloody Sundays / listen to what happens / to an accent / when no-one wants it / inverted vowels dance! *A pound to climb the tower / she was looking in the mirror* / sorry / we don't have room / sorry / you can look / through the Gate / at our received pronunciation / marvel at us / postcode lottery / makes competition entry possible / but / *We're sorry / we couldn't understand you / what is a mammy / a PSNI / a provisional IRA?*

London / are you Gatekeeper? / melting pot London / melting pot an open gate / the circuit / well named / is circular / all change and you / do the one / he did last month / she's doing next month / we are all Brixton / Hackney / Shoreditch / Old Street / London Bridge /

London Bridge lets people in / London Bridge is falling down / the Gate stands strong / open mic two minutes long / we prioritise regulars / can't really make space / for tourists   *What have you done?   What have you won? That's Irish. What have you won in London?*

Nationwide, in your eagerness to showcase a cross-section of UK-wide spoken word talent you travelled as far afield as...
Birmingham.

Imposter Syndrome / are you Gatekeeper? Do you keep me? You are small voice / not at all voice / let me have fun voice / only sting when I try to run voice / when I try to fly voice / only shout / when it's for my own good voice / *what did I tell you?* voice / it's your own choice voice / Gate is open but you know / what will happen / if you try to go through voice / told you so voice / lack of talent voice / keep small voice / be safe / no harm / ever came / to anyone who stayed safe / minded their manners and their business / smiled and applauded Shakespeare plays / took a day as a tourist / Dublin are doing these James Joyce days / drink it all in / then go home / be small / foetal / curl into cushion / and your destiny can be cushion / sat on / squashed / school-teacher voice echoes from above / recommending a career choice in IT / you have the right / quiet nature for it

Somewhere though / you found a key / and you don't know / what it means / but you found a *key* / it must fit / in here somewhere / you jiggle it / a little and the queue forms / behind you / sighing / glancing at watches / we haven't got all day / can you just let us past? / it's not us really /   it's these Gates they / clang shut / at the same time every night / you only get in if / you've earned the right / through an accident of birth / a miracle at best / and you don't want a miracle / you want only to impress / for that they need to listen / for that they need to open / so you keep on jiggling that old key / and you keep on doing that hoping / 'cos you're not here / to be quiet / you came here to be outspoken / unbroken / not token / eloquent / you are meant / to open

Villain (iv)

The video circulates, as familiar as Rain Man
counting cards, counting   cards.
But this is the first time I've seen hands move
in exactly that way.
Not self-beratingly or hurrying
along a thinking process.
Just... relaxation.
Being.

                            It's dancing

Enema Redux

In which The Cockroach goes deeper

You must do this one-handed.
You cannot lie on your back,
you cannot lie on your front,
you lie on your left and
don the plastic glove, shake the bottle vigorously
for 30 seconds,
turn the nozzle 180 degrees
                and insert.

It is the left side for a reason:
the anus becomes the rectum
becomes the colon
on the left side. The cool
liquid, the healing liquid
will travel this passageway
and bathe the ulceration
for the ten minutes you have
been instructed to lie there
then turn to your right side
so the medicine can blaze a trail
across to the right side colon
and trickle down towards the small bowel.
This is not an enema to prompt expulsion.
There is no rushing, knock-kneed to the toilet.
This is topical application of medication
to heal the sores and as such
it is in your best interest to retain
the liquid as long as possible. It is ideal
if this is the last thing you do before bed

and attempt to hold it until morning
when some leftover will escape:
a whitish stain on morning stools.

Villain (v)

For all the books made about mental illness,
for all case studies on neurodivergence,
for all films in which we seek out motivation
— why is protagonist the way he is
(protagonist is always He)? —
examination has never gone into the dances,
although they are many, and they repeat endlessly.

And I remember dancing when   exciting things!
joy filled me   had to spill out
I would use my voice shrilly,
for   release!
I would leap   cross a room
— not remembering the action of crossing —
using my hands to propel the happiness,
or to release it,
or to sustain it.

The Beast Approaches: A Tragedy In Ten House Parties

InwhichInwhichInwhichInwhichInwhichInwhichInwhichInw

1.

T says
she has a plan
when they are together next
she will leave *marks*
she will approach his girlfriend in the toilets
with details of mark placement
he will be caught!
and we laaaaaaugh

                                              2.

                                          L says
                                  it's a long story
                          but when he was with R
                              she became pregnant
            (somehow, immaculately, anonymously)
                      He would not get involved
                      but M travelled with her
                            M is so kind
                          She is with M now
                             He hates M

3.

You receive a MySpace friend request from him
You have never spoken
His profile offers you no intellectual stimulation
No HTML
You deny the request

4.

S is at the party
somewhat the worse for wear
She doesn't party often
usually has a reason
usually has an incentive
a prize
her jeans so low you can see wisps of pubic hair
peeking over the waistband
I don't know why she bothers,
C says
he's not that nice

5.

At A's house
on Hallowe'en
we are painting
spiderwebs up her arms
she rolls her eyes when someone mentions him
Oh, him
dismissively

6.

Hiding in N's bedroom
as everyone is too... keyed up
talk turns to P
He's lovely! N says
Looks a little like you-know-who
But nicer
Much nicer

7.

He asks you
why you didn't accept his friend request
you said you didn't know him
and his profile wasn't very decked out
He laughs
says he will ask again in the future
sometime
it is the first time you have spoken

8.

There are five of you at the party
one leaves, one sleeps
three are left and you are all singing, singing
this is a competition
you and he have strong voices
and knowledge of these songs
and are peacocking
R is more gentle
and you have a choice

He disappears, and by default you will choose R
but when R goes to the bathroom
the other reappears
(has he been waiting?)
and it is exciting
this pulling by the arm
this up the stairs
you are used to the pull and the drag
and it is done

9.

E is more shocked at your shock
than at your story
But that's...
everyone knows
He's known for that
Hadn't you heard?

10.

You ask T
if he ever hurt her
and she looks exasperated for a second
because you are being sensitive again
but she says yes
that he could be... aggressive
she just didn't want to rock the boat

she says yes

Intermission/Larvae

*On telling a friend I am writing to an insect theme and
finding out months later she has assumed I meant maggots*

But Maggots do not cross my mind at all:
the plump rot-seeking them of single mind.
Fat little white and wriggling shits with gall,
but Maggots do not cross my mind at all.
First time you found a dead bird, held in thrall,
turn over corpse, the bird's eye sockets blind.
But Maggots do not cross my mind at all;
the plump rot-seeking them of single mind.

Death should be still, not undead, filled with things
which almost serve to stand the bird upright.
Excited bubbling underneath the wings;
death should be still, not undead, filled with things.
Beak opens for a squawk, this dead bird sings
a music jelly-filled, so moist, this blight.
Death should be still, not undead, filled with things
which almost serve to stand the bird upright.

Dreamboy

In which The Cockroach tries Fiction Therapy to lose herself in sweet narrative arcs

I don't love love. I like love, tolerate love, am a little sick of love. It's love that makes my eyes flick away for a millisecond when couples smooch on tv, telling myself it's normal to do this and cringe at the soft sucking sound of a kiss. Normal, not baggage, not issues not fear not utmost panic not *I don't want to be touched, I just want to be held.* Not gritting teeth and convincing myself with gallons of cranberry juice that I am well, adjusted, smooth, seamless, sexy, uncaring, nonchalant woman. I don't love love.

But these boys on my movie screen are glowing. Golden lion glowing and as soon as I start to warm to their sun, as soon as I start to gaze upon them their colour drains from them. There is a drowning, a knife, a skull fracture and I can love these safe boys but my love is killing them. Movie boys will always comb their hair and shoot themselves, will lose themselves in heavy-lidded meaningful eye contact before they plummet off the cliff. I cannot possibly be responsible for all of this and yet I am. The cutting room floor was different before I became involved. I am changing the cellular makeup of these narratives just by engaging. Five of us lie on a bed, gigging with legs woven through each other's and leather-jacket boy gazes down on us, black hair falling forward over his face. He is laughing, not unkindly, we feel safe but this will be the death of him. He is too tall somehow and I wonder how his face is created. How the bones and teeth of the skull scaffold the skin in a way that mine never did.

Lord, put me
to sleep again.
If I sleep I can
remake them. They
are Angels and
by their deaths
they are healing me.

Please, God: Netflix me another Angel.

The Rape of Solitaire

In which The Cockroach contemplates physical intimacy

I

The watching of a Bond film
is all Bond girl beauty,
Bond girl boldness. Bolshy,
brash, brave, buxom. All
except for Solitaire.

Solitaire turned her cards, read the future in stick men and Priestesses, where suns have eyes, the sky is yellow. King of Cups, Magicians theorise, Strength wrestles with a lion and The Fool is ready to amble off a cliff. The Fool is always a man. James Bond is a man, the man of all men, only likes the bold, brash, buxom Bond girls and as such, should not notice Solitaire at all. Priestess, Goddess, Empress and as such, she should not notice him; she should clutch her pentacle and close her eyes against him.

Our nation is united in our love for Bond. Moneypenny moons after him, he is surrounded by Pussy Galore, Honey Ryder. A different one each film and this is never quite justified. The implication is that he ignores Moneypenny because she is plain, secretary, brunette, but in truth, he ignores her because she is a constant. *Don't shit where you eat Bond,* you could get in trouble if you do so. You cannot abandon someone you are tied to, you cannot humiliate them like you can a gangster's moll: strip her naked, watch her without her knowing,

promise her always. She's a nice place to visit but you
wouldn't want to live there. He's a nice place to visit
but you wouldn't want to live there. Solitaire! Clutch
your pentacle and close your eyes, if you cannot see
him, he cannot win.

Did the Rape of Solitaire sit ill with anyone else?
Not a rape! They cry, she goes willingly,
knowing she will lose her power if she lies with him
or thinking she might lose her power if she lies with him
or thinking she might gain a partner if she lies with him.
Our most British man, our man to admire, switches the
cards and each she turns is TheLoversTheLoversThe
Lovers (there is only one in each deck). The fates are
telling her he is her destiny; he is not. He cheats. She's
a nice place to visit but he wouldn't want to live there.
Bond girls are naked, humiliated, discarded — if they
are very lucky destroyed in a hail of bullets — but she is
the only one who loses her power.

Sullied. Deflowered. Spoiled.
What is this virgin notion of clean, fresh flesh?
Why should a conscious choice spoil a girl?
Why, perhaps more worryingly, should a lack
of choice spoil a girl? That choice can be removed
but surely always flowering, always in bloom?
This is no ruining,
it is no magic wand.
Your power is all yours.

II

Imagine, then, growing up cursed.
Cursed with the bad magic
but the thought possesses you
that bad magic is still magic,
still being chosen by an entity
(and this entity must be discerning,
to stay with you for such a time.
Such a time, it feels like centuries)
to poison all the people nearby,
to Babel your innocent chatter
so that when it reaches ears it is foul,
blasphemy, the worst things any child
could ever say. People wisely stay away
and the child considers, because this child
is a considerer and changes what she says
and melts herself a little: speaks left-wise,
wax droplets running down her chin
as the wick burns down from the top
of her head, burbles wet words, spits
through the flame, wax congeals on lips.
She still appears merry; she has no idea
that there is infection here. No one can hear.
They hear what the demon wants them to hear
and the woman becomes a woman and learns silence.

Belfast vernacular: to get your head showered
(to take a break, to get away
from tiresome, trying things)
so the woman now a woman
takes things literally, places her head
under a running shower, puts out her blazing candle
and decides to live life dry.

Things are so much easier
if you're no longer melting:
you can taste your food
without that after-smell of burning,
you can say what you mean
and mean what you say.
The demon has mellowed
and just wants quiet at this time in his life.
They curl up together companionably:
husband and wife (Hammer Horror Bride).
If you are married to a demon,
if he stays with you faithful
you must be *special special special*
and he begs forgiveness, in his own way.
You cannot have relationships
but he will allow your words
to echo out, unfettered, unfiltered
when you speak to crowds.
Only on stage will you have any impact
and all of your life you have wanted to have impact.
If this is the price you must pay to be listened to
after so long silent you will pay it.
You will be this demon's possession
and when he offers you the deal,
you make your choice: closeness
with others or this gift of words?
You close your eyes and whisper fiercely
The gift the gift the gift.

Solitaire, you chose a plain man
with no magic and the demon left you.
What would you do if given the choice again?

Villain (vi)

Buffalo Bill gyrates to 'Goodbye Horses'
prepares his next victim
for the making of his skinsuit
prepares himself to   become.

Joker is shirtless and undulates,
velociraptor arms stick out   all
elbow
              angles
but precisely   where he
              wants   them
rib cage rises, falls
hangs starkly above a concave abdomen
hands present the claw,
the elegant cigarette holder,
the blowing of a kiss,
the beautiful dream,
the metamorphosis,
the becoming... when he is alone.

We see him breathe deeply and
rehearse the choreography
rehearse the choreography
rehearse the choreography —

The Hose, Again

In which The Cockroach was right all along, for all the good it did her

Do not be surprised by any of this;
you were clotheslined for this,
begged them for years to string you up
like a washing line:
endoscopy and colonoscopy together
— you on a hose —
they don't expect to find anything.
Gag reflex works overtime.
Hose meant to be
the thickness of an index finger
but when you see it
you realise they meant
the thickness of a man's index finger.
Your finger is mere chicken bone, man the default.
A nurse present whose only purpose
seems to be to stroke your hair,
ask questions to distract you,
compliment you on your hair colour choice,
lets you squeeze her hand during the biopsies,
the removal.
You, weak, are rolled on your back
and he looms over you.
They found something
synonymous with Colitis or Crohn's.
All this time they just thought you were sensitive!
Girls with their nervous stomachs
(best not to humour girls,
waste the hose on them).
Only men know what pain truly is.

Villain (vii)

We have seen him lose so much
make so many errors
that when he emerges from behind the curtain
with a precise triple turn on twinkle toes,
it is a triumph. He murders, yes,
gets arrested, yes
but holds a crowd of rioters transfixed
as he moves twistingly, teasingly
on the roof of a battle-scarred police car.
He has *become*.

Cockroach

Hannah Gadsby's 'Nanette'
is — Oh! — is devastating.
Is honest,
is a manual of what to write, how to write,
what not to write,
of criticism you will receive
when you write what you like.
Is first of all, a comedy show.
Speaks of tension
and relief because
you cannot have relief
without tension
without relief.
But the relief is... a lie?
A letting them down gently, a
laying them on soft cotton sheets, a fiction-
al twist in the tale to soothe.

Life is tension
unrelenting
only relieved when you tell someone
I'm fine
or *It isn't as bad as it looks!*
or *Let's talk about something else,*
you must be bored of my problems by now!

I could never be a comedian.
If a cockroach releases its tension it dies,
and I can't release all this tension, I've tried!

Cockroaches die on their backs,
legs curled up,
a force of hydraulic exoskeleton exertion combined
with the pushing of blood through their legs which
causes them to straighten.

Cockroaches die on their backs
old and weak,
find it harder to exert propulsion to force
their legs open.
One side may collapse, cause them to tip   over!

Cockroaches die on their backs.
Insecticides *zap*
affect their nervous system,
cause *zap* muscular spasms,
flip it on its back.

I lie on my back,
I lie on my back,
I wonder will I die on my back.
I'm not ready to talk about #metoo yet (I will be soon).
Can I project my voice as a dead thing?
Can I project my voice on my back?
Suzanne told us to project our voices
to the back of the room.
Her famous blue raincoat was
— *no*, this isn't about Cohen but it's Ireland,
we all had raincoats.

Brundlefly changed bit by bit;
significant to him the moments when his face fell off,
when he picked an ear up off the floor
and tossed it in the trash;

significant to me the moment he sat in a bar,
Brundlefly Barfly and arm wrestled a biker,
a man-mountain.
Fixed stare, arms locked,
I couldn't look, I couldn't look away,
I couldn't look, I couldn't look away.
I remembered for years
how he broke the arm of a bad man,
how he regurgitated his powers
on the arm of a bad man.
What would I do to the arms of a bad man?
I'm not ready to talk about #metoo yet (I will be soon).
He changed bit by decaying bit;
Gregor Samsa changed all at once;
both changed from men into something else.
Can I change from something Other
back into one of you?
Such a feat has not been documented yet.

Villain (viii)

Buffalo Bill longs to become; the Black Swan: to become.

Those two teenage girls in a bathtub in Christchurch, New Zealand: to become.

Slug

In which the unsuspecting Cockroach meets a squelching creature with no voice of its own

The man.
The man wore glasses and.
The optician wore glasses which I suppose
led to his interest in ophthalmology.
I never found out what led to his interest in music.
The optician said I could sing for them. Join them.
Me. Shy me!
Recite parrot-fashion the lyrics given to me.

Later.

The optician said
We would like you to contribute lyrics to our project
We would like you to   lyric
We would like you to contribute
We would like you
We   *like* you
And so I wrote.

You cannot say it feels like rape. You know this. There are things you cannot say even though every time someone shouts on Twitter 'I can say, because I have experienced both!' you think they might be right. You think they probably do know. You think you do know. You can only say there is a burning in your chest and you hold your breath. You hold your breath and wait for the drop. His name is the drop. Libraries are the drop. Peeling sweet oranges on the street drops drops drops. Your stomach has no bottom and things fall of it. Your self-esteem falls out. Your courage falls out. Your desire to work in partnership creatively is in freefall. Your mouth is full of bad man's tongue licking up your words and bitches should not speak with their mouths full. Full-fat slug is warm and pitted, full-fat slug is singing, singing. You are discredited as mental illness girl. Mental illness girl tells lies. Mental illness girl cannot write, why would we plagiarise her? Opticians, much like slugs, have long careers in the music industry and this is the proof that they can do the writing. They do not need your scribblings, girl.

And a city believed him. Reader, you gaze upon the words of someone who cannot write like a man can. Don't you?

Villain (ix)

He captivates all the little incel boys, crying
to Mommy but we mustn't be so reductive,
because he also captivates me. I see myself,
trudging home, shoulders hunched, clutching
paper bag filled with medications. And just
before bed, he settles with Mother to watch
their favourite show... just as I do.

A painting of a loser is vivid
perhaps never quite so vivid
until witnessed by another loser.

I find myself on the margins, closer to the edge
than I would ever like to admit, at most four
people away from falling off entirely.

But we try to forget.
We TV show,
medicate,
clowning-ly try to forget.

      We dance.

When is a Body not a Body?

In which The Cockroach plays Twenty Questions

(vegetable)

Dear weak machine/Dear soft food diet/Dear dizzy spell/Dear restless legs/Dear allergic reaction/Dear eye twitch/Dear moisture deficit/Dear voice rasp/Dear food reflux/Dear raised welt/Dear shoulder regret/Dear digestion refusal/Dear lingering carbuncle/Dear Prozac sweats /Dear blood drool/Dear grinding cogs/Dear slipped alignment/Dear orgasm cramp/Dear spotted tissue/Dear cracked vibrato/Dear sodden poultice/Dear heart   beat

(mineral)

Dear accessible cubicle/Dear physio tape/Dear yoga, once/Dear dance floor(ed)/Dear needle nurse/Dear ergonomic chair/Dear lost friends/Dear romantic memory/Dear hose wielder/Dear dry crackers/Dear fizzing electrolytes/Dear queer contemplation/Dear foil dish/Dear future hope/Dear hereditary failure/Dear spiralling history

(animal)

Dear faint buzzing/Dear sponging mouthparts/Dear compound eyes/Dear segmented legs/Dear veined wing/Dear thirsty proboscis/Dear 21-day cycle/Dear pest control

Snake, Seductive

The Last Temptation of Cockroach

My ancient reptilian brain insectile awakens,
ponders potential transformation.
Sssssssssnake is all thingssss.
Snake says if I sacrifice solitary,
cold blood can sizzle.
I can ssssing in the sssun!
My ssself-esssteem will wind back years
to before the shellshock,
before you stood in the sea surrounded
and screamed as it swept against ankles.

Be still as starfish.
Cease the snivelling!

For forty days and nights
I stayed in the desert with Snake,
who showed me what I could be.
Could be slim, smug, sassy girl,
celebrated shiny hair, slip of a thing
surrounded by sycophants.
Sally-Sarah-Sue goes to soirees, sips champagne,
sexes sexy Simon,
sleeps, speaks,
sees only what is straight in front of her.
Office secretary.
Supine spine.
Sarah's skin is soft; smokes, suppurates. She suffers.

I tap my sleek, strong shell.
I lie on my back, I will not die on my back.
Cockroach will not be supine.

Snake is enemy, is Wolf.
They all have different tactics:
Snake simpers, convinces;
Wolf wears a friend-disguise,
keeps Cockroaches close as enemies.
None of them understand
the hydraulic nature of my exoskeleton!

Keep the tension in my legs.
Keep the tension, keep the tension.
If you want a release
of the tension you're at the wrong show!
My legs remain strong.

Becoming

Butterfly

Francis Dollarhyde
is becoming beautiful.
Do you see? You must.

Villain (x)

The loner:
pictured here in his natural habitat
(often grotty, grubby, lit by a single hanging bulb,
various shades of brown,
a place no-one else would choose)
prepares for the kill
(there is always a kill).
dons gloves and luxuriates   soft velvet
precision of finger finding   slot!
Slicks back hair to music of choice,
throws off the shackles of loner
completes the dance   mating ritual
with himself
He is ready
This accurate representation
you win awards for
playing the freak convincingly
nominated for going so   far!
outside comfort zone
Show the general public a peek
behind the carnival curtain,
just a little one.
The freak summons power and then uses it to harm.
Why else would power be required?

Today, I thought of Eyam

In which The Cockroach experiences Her Year of Great Healing

>   Mother hurts herself
>   washing her hands too much, far
>   far too much, they crack.

I utilise driveways on my walks.
We see each other approach
at a distance; we stiffen.
If we can take it wide we do, large circles
around each other. Walk on
an increasingly quiet road.
Sometimes one crosses to avoid me
and I sing their praises!
Some will blunder ever closer
and this is not a game of chicken;
I do not want to win it,
I lurk in driveways.
If they want the right of way so badly,
this diseased, shining path,
they are welcome to it.

*

Nightmares of the plague days:

You are walking alone
along a deserted street.
Streets should be deserted; this is welcome.
A group of teenagers appear and you try not to
think of them as:
wild teenagers,

unwelcome teenagers,
feral.

You walk closer and one coughs - he has a cough!
You cannot veer away because this is a dream
and your options are limited. You fear
turning back in case you attract their attention.

As you are abreast with them,
head down, following all the rules
he draws back and spits in your face.
For 48 hours after the dream you stay indoors,
too frightened to venture out.

*

The suicides will fall into three categories

Did you hear that a woman in a supermarket
started biting people in the queue?
A man paid for groceries with many coins
but before handing them to cashier
he placed each one inside his mouth
and then gifted it, spittle-shining, to her,
to capitalism. Security removed him
because even capitalism has limits (does it?)
but that image will stay with her for the rest of her life:
Coin-metal mouthed man, pennies for teeth,
grinning at her and asking her
to accept his moist generosity

The first category of suicides will be the scared

Five days ago Mavis cleared her throat

and you haven't felt right since.
There is a burning in your throat,
your chest. It could be angina.
A man walked so close to you,
you said 'Please move away'.
He did not move away. You cannot
stand this death-watch. Death rates.
Every time you receive an online
notification it is death rates. You snap
elastic bands on your wrists
repeatedly, they leave marks.
It is not enough.

*

I find myself in the graveyard.
Needing quiet company,
needing the quietest of companions.
From my high vantage point
I can see all around, no-one
can sneak up on me. A man
wheels a pram up and down the hills.
It is not a relaxing day out
with child, he is pushing for something.
He leans into the incline, head down,
arms out straight in front of him.
Pram as battering ram.
Pram as cardio aid.
Baby as excuse to work out
this stifling, indoor rage.

*

The second category will be the lonely

Lonely does not mean what you think it means.
Hundreds, thousands of people at the touch of a key
but are any of them speaking to you
directly? Do they revolve around you?
Did you know not everyone has internet access?
You start to have trouble
sleeping, the words
you are not using
bubble up inside you.
You gasp for breath,
this house air
is not fresh air.
You smell your own sweat,
legs are restless and jiggling.
Where is the line
between stimulated and overstimulated?
Your eyes are open, your mind is flayed open,
no-one to sing it soothed and closed.

*

There are more living, walking people
here, all blessedly far apart.
A small family reads inscriptions on gravestones.
A couple walk hand-in hand at the North East end.
I walk the smaller paths
and in this dead end of places,
some of these paths are dead ends.
I pick my way between gravestones, respectfully.
I will always walk this land respectfully,
greeting those who lie underneath
with a whispered song.

I spend my time with the Orrs, the McMasters,
the Campbells and thoughts drift to Eyam.

When we were 12 years old
in school, we read of Eyam.
We dipped letters written in our best calligraphy
in tea and toasted them to make them look olde.
We read aloud in class and this was —
we all agreed — the dullest
book we had ever experienced.
A dry cough of a book
until I took it home and it lived!
The characters lived,
until they died
in this village,
this Eyam-place,
 when the plague came
they made the only choice,
the Corona choice,
the modern choice,
the choice even then in 1666, a pact
to not leave those village boundaries
until the fever raged no more.
If anyone left, they would carry
to others and the spread
could be limitless so for a year
it fed on them, choice cuts on a market stall,
discarding some and gorging on others
with seeming randomness
until the filth was buried,
goiters subsided, boils lanced,
fevers broken, whole families
no more than carvings on stone.
Today I thought of Eyam.

*

The third category will be the NHS

Have you seen them crying
on the news broadcasts?
Have you clapped uselessly for them?
They intubate the foaming mouths
and struggling lungs close enough
to bathe in the carbon dioxide you expel.
The ladies of the Women's Institute gamely swap
their knitting patterns for the sewing of masks
humming Jerusalem all the while.
They will not sew enough,
could not possibly sew enough
for all the doctors in this green and pleasant land,
their feet in present time aching
and raw from 14 hour shifts.
They will not cease
from mental fight, until they do.
Nor shall their gloves
slip from their hand
(that is the last pair).
I do not mention the nurses
for they have not been counted
and if they choose to leave
on their own terms, they will
not be counted among official statistics.

Did you perhaps wait two weeks
for your last GP appointment, in 2019?
You will wait longer
after their numbers have been decimated.

Sister tells us of
conspiracy theories.
We place hands o'er ears!

*

To escape, we must walk.
We must go to still places and breathe deeply:
a half-remembered jaunt
decades ago, a duck pond
that I never found again
and I will find it, this time.

I do not but
I find a magic place.

Gate nothing more than a space
between posts and I step over:
grass is long and silent.
This place is *thin*
and as I breathe the thin air
I take note of the wildlife all around me.

Mr Squirrel! Pay no mind to me,
I am just a sweaty human.
Mr Squirrel, you don't want me.

I walk deeper
through what I see now is a meadow.
Teens have had a bonfire here, perhaps
many fires. These teens, being real,
causing fires should also cause fear
but there is no fear in this thin place.
A discarded bottlecap shines up

at me and screams
Corona Extra!
Isn't it just? I say,
Bottlecap, you're so right.

I hear humans now. The bounce
of a ball but they are far away;
sound carries in these thin places.
They are across the river and I can stand still,
actually stand still, fearing no trespassers
and stare into the moving water, this offshoot of

River Lagan, it has been a month
since I have seen you. We have never before
been separated for such a duration.
I will not leave it so long again.
Today I thought of Eyam
but even Eyam's siege ended.

Have people before emerged from waters shining?
The hands, submerged endlessly
are eventually cleansed and dried,
soothed with hand cream and treated
like princesses. A baptism of sorts.
My eyes gleam.

In years to come I'll celebrate tree roots,
the comic crunch of acorns underfoot
and I slowly walk the path toward home.

Villain (xi)

But others need to summon.
To leave the house,
to break the mental spirals
we summon. Those of us
who walk powerless,
who feel the on/off switch
as a drain on our resources need to
ration the days we switch it on.

For those days we switch it on,
we use ritual,
we use masks,
we use dance.

You might see a subtle skip,
a heel kick turn, a flourish which will,
you can be assured,
be continued in the privacy of home.

Blood/Dogs

In which The Cockroach contemplates the ouroboric nature of 'O'... and Bob

                     dog
            good dog doggy
      good   boy
      dog   good
              dog
     doggy   boy
     soothe   boy
              dog
    slow   words
    bloom   knows of
     horror   drools
       dog boy tooth
          blood

      dogs smell fear
fear smog smell floods nostrils
     makes them feel alive!
   don't show palm of hand
     show flat of hand
    flat of hand soothes
    says I come in peace
   approach with caution
   come slowly to dog
        but no
     dog not good
    dog blood thirst
     blood fiend
you show flat of hand but
      dog knows

dog knows of horror
nose of horror
horror odour clings, lingers
dog drools over cloying spoor
dog knows you not cool, not strong
you'll not fool dog boy dog!
dog storms your fortress
blood dog blood

audiences smell fear
show them the flat of your hand
show them the palm of your hand
show them the arc of your fourth position
they can still scent you
knock kneed rehearsing
hands shaking
she looks... nervous
she looks less
we are distinctly
unimpressed

slow clap
look! gobby
not so gobby now
not so gobby cow
storybook shook
story flogs horse
shouts, moody, shakes
pouts, makes
enemies
makes audiences ill at ease
audiences smell fear

s'cos:

look! Bob!
observe Bob
obs. Bob
obvs.
Bob shouts! bravado
bravo
Bob commands, not gobby
Bob smoothly controls crowd
Bob holds crowd in palm of hand
not flat of hand
Bob shouts, stony
not phony
not broody
not bloody womb
boobs
Bob's work is good storm
book-worthy
Bob's words glow
cool
Bob is showstopper!

oh, look
hoor still here
hoor skulks
stop shouting, God!
stop gobbing
hormonal
slow down
bloody womb
shhhh
Bob's on!

she shakes
audiences smell fear

what can she do to quell fear?
audience creates fear
but she is, above all, still here
cos gobby, ok
hormones flood
monthly blood
but look! story
look! love
look! glory
look! above the knock kneed terror
horror of dog drooling
cold of dog's tooth
there'll be no fooling
dog boy dog crowd dog
but womb hoor boobs has a story
womb hoor boobs has a truth
grotty slob isn't boring
and grotty slob's got the proof

Bob?
stop
cos yr not
yr boy blown
over by storm
moon womb
blood & boobs
may cry
may shake
may fear
may break
may horror of crowds
shy close door
but goes on
cos story glows

Bob shouts
but Moon Womb's
story *glows*.

Three Fictional Women Meme

In which The Cockroach chooses role models who are widely considered to be unconventional

In the 90s
women thought they were all Bridget Jones.
All I cannot resist him!
I cannot use my instinct to see who is bad for me.
I smoke, I cannot use my common sense
to know this is bad for me.
I cannot remember last night and cannot use
my doctor's advice to know this is bad for me.

I vomit after a night out.
I vomit after a big meal.
I am having a wonderful time.

I have accidents and fall over,
so clumsy we fell into bed,
I shrank my sweater in the wash,
I am lovable because of this.

I do not have accidents;
I have deliberates.
Which three fictional women am I?
The internet asked me because it wants to know!
The internet laughs at us
because it thinks we are all Bridget Jones.

First, I choose Carrietta N. White.
Carrie White.
Carrie.
May you develop the power

to defend yourself eventually, spectacularly.
After the first blooding, alone and in water
you scream and beg for help.
No help is offered,
no help will ever be offered.
After the second blooding,
gratuitously in public:
to cause such chaos you must
cut a pig exactly right, slit
carotid artery, drain the gilt clean
and catch in a bucket the drowning liquid.
They are all going to laugh at you but, blessedly
they are all going to stop.
They will stop because you make them.
Focus on a single lightbulb first:
when it catches afire
the sensors alert the sprinkler system
and everyone is still laughing! Wet,
dancing in the indoor rain,
slippery teenage skin,
dresses cling to upright nipples.
They do not realise yet
until water shorts electricity
running through live sound equipment;
a guitar bursts into flame.
(You have been practicing!)
Like lemmings they move as a wave
as one towards a door
that takes at most two at a time.
The animals flee two by two until
a force as hard as carbon,
a door as closed as reinforced steel.
Lock the door, throw away the key,
let them fry.

I choose Lisbeth Salander.
I choose mathematics,
cool crisp numbers in the cool clean snow
all slotting exactly into place.
If you can control the numbers
you can control the world.
I choose unconventional friendships
forged in unusual, pressured circumstances:
people who will come to my aid when I call
because they know
I do not call often;
I barely call at all.
I choose the secrets behind the internet screen
when the lights are low in a dark basement
you can get to know
people far beyond a coffee morning
— beyond ladies who lunch —
when they are incognito and when you are Wasp.
I choose vacationing by myself:
watch the beach sunset on a terrace,
my house the way I want my house
the way I need my house.
I choose biding my time, because we
are not always strong at the moment of action,
because we all experience lows
and it is up to us how we deal with them.
I choose carving your crimes into your chest.
You will be reminded in the mirror,
in the shower. Oh no!
This will affect your ability to meet women!
Be glad your crimes were not carved on your face.

I choose Scarlett O'Hara.
I choose a me-first sensibility.

I choose desiring and desired,
rejecting what I don't desire,
having the right to make my choices,
having the courage to enjoy the right,
having the privilege to revel in my courage.
Knowing what I want want want.
Saying want three times,
saying want endlessly,
mouth open, luscious and pointing towards the excess
and in the absence of the excess
(in the absence of anything much)
and in the presence of monsters
I will make the monstrous decisions
to keep myself safe,
to keep those I love safe
because I do not love easily
or necessarily well
— in your understanding of the word well —
but I love bloody
and messily
and gaspingly.
You will end up a little scarred;
perhaps some bald patches
as you are wrenched from the drowning sea
by the hair;
you might lose unnecessary extremities
such as fingers, children or hangers-on
but you can feast with me at my table:
drink a toast to the rumours and the spreaders,
cast off our mourning in clothes of red,
throw our heads back
and laugh.

Villain (xii)

I searched for my grace in Hollywood
and all I got
was this lousy serial killer!

Swan/Suddenly/Suzanne

In which The Cockroach remembers kindnesses from wingèd Visionaries

Not everyone is Cockroach, is Snake.
I met a Swan once;
of all places, at a poetry slam.
Swan had never been to a poetry slam before
and as she spoke of many things
and spread her wings to soar
she sacrificed herself to the gods of the stopwatch
and read for five minutes,
meaning that I came first.
But more importantly I had made a friend.
But more importantly I made an ally
and this Swan who etched painful words
of the past
and the in-between
and old Ireland
and new Ireland
which co-exist,
who took my breath away with her wingspan whiteness
was simultaneously made breathless by... me?
And became encourager and protector.
Said you, Cockroach
have a voice that needs to be heard.
You, Cockroach have words.
You, Cockroach have a story to be told and many stories
that you haven't even begun to tell yet.
You must get your stories out there.
You must begin
to submit
to journals.

You have a gift.
A gift.

Suzanne said that too.

Suzanne was pretty
and we had never had a pretty teacher before.
Our teachers were the Roald Dahl quote:
A person who has good thoughts cannot ever be ugly. You can have a wonky nose and a crooked mouth and a double chin and stick-out teeth, but if you have good thoughts it will shine out of your face like sunbeams and you will always look lovely.

Our teachers were good thoughts
that shone like sunbeams,
our teachers were kindness.

First teacher knew I could not talk to others.
Did not know why (and nor did I)
but let me stand with her at break,
so I would not be alone.
Second teacher fed me books
when I finished my work early,
 books when I finished my work best.

In second class by second teacher I was encouraged
to share sketches with ~~the audience, sorry,~~ my class
and many days my ~~worshippers, sorry,~~ class
were told to down pens and watch what I had created
in my head, using a plastic teapot as a prop that was not
supposed to be a teapot but was supposed to be a dog,
or the meaning of life, or a tree.

Smalltown teachers talk to each other, speak highly

of those who imagine a teapot to be a delicious cake
and my teapot and I were taken under another wing.
First teacher and second teacher had wonky teeth
and double chins and glasses but could never be ugly.
Suzanne was third teacher and Suzanne was the first
pretty teacher we had. We learned her name through
*Miss! Miss! You're pretty Miss! What age are you Miss!! Miss!
Do you have a boyfriend? Miss! What's your name Miss what's
your name Miss what's your name?*

And — something almost unheard of — she answered
and — something almost unheard of — she liked us and
— something almost unheard of — she cared.

Suzanne taught us / to project our voices / to the back
of the room / Suzanne taught us / we were more than
/ the span of our arms / than the reach of our height /
we were the reach of our voices / and although we were
small / we were scared / we were seven years old /
our voices could command / an entire room / and she
taught me / my small voice / in this class of 25 / was the
loudest / that I had the most lines / the most
responsibility / and I would wear it well / I would
project well / that comfort zones / were in fact prisons /
we create for ourselves out of fear

7 was ruled by Suzanne / who / by being herself / taught
me / what a woman could be / who by being the woman
she was / listened and let me be myself / I did not find
my voice / so much as / find the people to listen to it

6 was learning of the existence of humour / 7 was mastering it / 7 was moving away / from the things I could
not do / the solitary easel / 7 pushed the easel over and

left / red poster paint footprints on the lino / 7 talked to people / 7 created a monster / a demon for attention / a Gollum / craving your applause / 7 seeks audience / 7 rejects your rejection / 7 only wants your GSOH 7 defines your GSOH / as laughing at her jokes / (7 is right) / 7 tastes power / 7 makes allies / a skill she never had before / a skill she rarely has again / Suzanne creates an eclipse / the planets align / 7 and Suzanne co-exist as familiars / 7 black cat struts over to you / sure of your acceptance / 7 is lucky and if you are lucky / she will cross your path / 7 eats your fear / 7 glows / 7 has strong legs and sturdy opinions / 7 has uncombed hair / 7 projects her voice to the back of the room / because Suzanne told her to / because Suzanne was right / because Suzanne was Witch / because Suzanne was God / because Suzanne married and changed her name / because Suzanne emigrated to the land of opportunity / and at 7 you can't remember her new name / if you ever knew it / because Suzanne only exists / now in your memory / if she ever existed at all

Villain (xiii)

I am no Buffalo Bill.

But I have been filled my whole life with the electric desire to move. Happy or sad. Happy is more graceful, certainly but a foot jiggling is a foot jiggling, restless legs and restless arms keep a body awake despite the emotion that inspired them and the urge to propel a head repeatedly into a wall, to shake out the bad thoughts, to dig nails into hands, to clench, to hit, to cancel the hurt is that same sharks on the carpet urge. The floor is lava the thoughts are good and I can fly now. My strides are seven leagues long, my hands reach for you gracefully and I arch foot to begin coming into my power. The dance can disconnect, is disconnect itself, it is the automatic on/off switch and it is both on and off coexisting. It is how we transcend manual to automatic. All arms and instinct, extended stim. We feel our grace even if you do not see it as such, if you tell us we are awkward. We stumble in your eyes.

The Writing Workshop as Place of Misunderstanding

In which The Cockroach attempts to begin the journey of justifying her own words

When the women at the writing workshop say your trauma
poem isn't believable because of the language
used by the characters and say you cannot blame
him for being like that because he was clearly
a teenager, because they were all clearly teenagers
and you say he was nearly thirty and they say
thirty year olds don't talk like that or they say
that no thirty year olds they ever hung out with
spoke like that, that they only hung out with
people who spoke eloquently and you realise
they have never experienced club culture
and you realise they do not want to experience
club culture and you realise experiencing club culture
may have damaged you and you wonder
who you would have been without club culture
and you wonder if you would be able
to hear pins drop without club culture
and you wonder if you would still be friends
with those people if they hadn't started dealing
and you admit to yourself you weren't bothered
by the dealing as much as the fact it made them
too busy to hang out and the people
at the writing workshop are good people,
they just prefer quiet nights in with books
and you yourself enjoy quiet nights in with books
but those nights need something to balance
them out, need screaming when the song,
that song starts and those nights need

only being able to make heavy-lidded eye contact
on a dancefloor when without music
you cannot look at anyone and you realise
the writing workshop is not your place,
not really but it is a means to an end
and what is this end really when you could be
breathing sweat and what is sweat really
when you could be breathing possibilities
and what are possibilities when they are carefully
debated by the writing workshop and you go home
and realise they were victim blaming, the whole group
was victim blaming and you are stronger
than all of them put together and you put
some music on in your kitchen and

                          you
                                      dance

Misophonia

In which The Cockroach hears all frequencies simultaneously

It starts   with silence,

    floating

                  in the black

        unstructured

                          void

hair not   bound   by   gravity

Make manifest.
Make manifest.
You can make anything in this state.
You can corn dolly their hearts,
twist them like straw,
set intentions like love potions.
You forgot what parts of you were for
until this,
until your eyes remember how to bathe-warm-glow,
until you gaze at something that suffers softly.
Eye contact is a choice you mostly reject
and yet,
and yet,
some eyes are pinwheel kaleidoscope starshine
and you must stare.
Remember who you are.
Remember who you are.

Two magicians, both alike in dignity.
They believe,
    they beckon,
        they balance,
    they bother,
they bellow,
    they bitter,
        they better,
    each other.
They butter
    each other.
        They smother
    each other.

A trickster god laughs, a high-pitched giggle
over almost before you catch it
and you are upturned in your dizziness.
it is a nauseating lurch.

(worm)

worm asks
May I eat you?
and you say *No?*
No.
No! A fierce no,
the only possible answer
but worm is not asking you.
worm is asking your confidence and it
rolls over,
        supplicant.
                So digestible,
an unformed thing
so baby raw, so new.

A pâté.
worm opens maw and un   la   forward
                            du   tes

taking in the m o r e of you,
barely even having to chew.

This is its favourite meal.

You carry worm
and worm carries you.
It is not symbiotic
though it may seem so,
though it may seem that worm is you.
worm is external,
worm is all the voices ever,
worm is all the punishments
that you ever gave yourself.
worm is the straw that breaks your back, repeatedly
but you still let it climb aboard,
call all aboard.
You are the captain of this.
You are the host.

worm is noise.
warm is chaos.
worm is misophonia,
constant chittering,
an underlying buzz,
is mocking laughter
is the sweet wrapper in the hands of the fidgeter
is the car alarm at 3am
is your neighbour singing
your favourite song out of tune

is rats under floorboards
is mocking you, is mocking you
is the frantic whispered Catholicism
underneath the soundtrack
is the child-adult voice singing dark lullabies
is just the radiator cooling, you tell yourself
you tell   yourself
you   tell   yourself
Your ears hurt most on days like this;
it is the wriggling.
It is so baby-screaming loud!

worm
      worm
            worm

Why do you let yourself be eaten up like this?
Like so much chew toy, like so much waste product.

You can do anything.
You castle bitch, you ivory tower,
you carving, you statue, you ICON .
You, Jadis of Charn.
You, Song of Susannah.
You red-headed twins: Mekare, Maharet.

Do not consort with low-born   worm.
Do not seek approval of   worm.
Do not attempt to befriend   worm.
Do not waste your breath on   worm.
Do not let the words of   worm   change you.
Do not allow   worm   to.
worm needs you more than you need worm.
worm fears you more than you fear worm.

You are to be feared.
More than that,
you are to be loved.
Open your eyes!
Remember who you are
and float.

It always starts
with silence.

To Elizabeth, Crying Uncontrollably in the Next Stall

After Kim Addonizio

Listen. You have never been a ghost. If you have
ever felt like ghost-behind-glass it is time to smash
the window. You live plainly, yet you have the specks
of electric blue glitter underneath your fingernails,
embedded so deeply you have forgotten it is there. You
are the one who found the best song on the worst night
of your life and kept it close, so that night would be
worth something. You are the one who makes
every night worth something. These people
are not afraid of you; they are in shock. When you feel
you are being swallowed by *the nothing* say my name
Bastian! Or speak your own. There are two magicians.
There have always been two magicians and *whisper it*
they do not like each other but these magicians have
always both been you. Go to the desert with a cup
and make your own hourglass, you alone can decide
how much time it will hold. Community is coming.
It smells like ordinary, like reward, like cigarette
smoke and ink, like a summer day in the park.
Use your eyes. Yes, they look at things: this is
a thing and that is a thing but set them to laser
sometimes, to see what comes of the burning.
It will be a surprise. Do not envy the woman
with the rasp of a crow. She is trapped. You
are luminous. Place a lightbulb between your lips
and it will look dim by comparison. Place a
lightbulb between your lips and it will shatter
from the power surge. You are the power surge.

When you sleep you levitate. Small creatures hold you up with tiny claws. Is joy coming? Fuck that. It is already here.

Three Fictional Women Meme (ii)

In which The Cockroach watches the DVD deleted scenes and extras, including the Director's commentary

These women are cockroaches. And do you scream and lift your skirts above your ankles at that? Do you require a trigger warning? These creatures are disgusting, you cry. You once experienced an infestation. You once were overrun. Your little white town overrun with melanin strangers. If a teacher slows down for the slowest pupil in the class the others will be held back. Their bright and shining stars will tarnish. That building cannot be fitted with a ramp because it is protected and must be kept just so. Do a virtual tour.

Shall I sanitise my language? Shall I say these women are *different*, or perhaps praise them with masculine traits? Say they have balls, say they are unique, mathematical, say they are deficient in friendliness, or empathy, or understanding. They have the focus of a scientist, of a man beyond their years. They can take care of themselves in a most unfeminine way and this we do not admire (though there is much to admire). We analyse their coldness and make them specimens. We other them so do not be squeamish. Let them cockroach. Let them cling to rocks while others fall. Let them be better than you, and achieve, and last longer. Carve their names in rock, these scuttling, surviving women. Make monuments to them. They control their own tension while you release and die. Do not denigrate them. But if you do, I know why.

Keep us as bobble-headed soft-bellied Bridget Joneses. That is safer, isn't it?

Villain (xiv)

But on careful inspection, I was elsewhere too. I was The Breakfast Club's Judd Nelson fistpumping to Simple Minds after a sweet kiss. I was Stand By Me's 'Lollipop, Lollipop' train-track, cheek-popping; the Risky Business sock-floor slide. I was carrying a watermelon to see the boy I liked in Dirty Dancing. Because these movements are there, but when storylined with joy, neurotypical society see themselves. They see themselves in joy as they believe and have been reared to believe they are entitled to these interactions. They recognise the story. They triumph while we are othered.

But it is all the dance.

In an attempt to try and redirect your unhealthy lockdown parasocial obsession with the poet

In which The Cockroach basks in the warm glow of the soft bisexual lighting

Send your Harry Styles videos, your *Watermelon Sugar*. Send your Michael Hutchence documentaries. Send your Peaky Blinders boxsets with the blessed glowing skull of Cillian Murphy. Send your Strictly Come Dancing Samba and Pasodoble perfect tens. Send your dirty, riding Dublin Soul! Send your Cinema Paradiso montages. Send your Byzantine immortal Saoirse Ronans. Send Lestat. Send Sky Masterson, no, an assortment of Brandos. Send Heathers. Send your Mikkelsen devouring a stomach. Send Gomez and Morticia doing the Tango. Send your Aubrey Beardsley illustrations. Send Salome with the head of John the Baptist. Send your Adam Driver singing Sondheim with tears in his eyes. Send your Camomile Lawn. Send Al Pacino's ever-widening eyeballs in The Godfather. Send Quadrophenia. Send your Choose Life. Send your Atomic. Send your Sally Rooney will-they-won't-they will-they-won't-they-will-they-won't-they Connell and Marianne, Jesus! Send your Heavenly Creatures bathtub. Send your Umbrellas in Cherbourg, the height of Deneuve's beauty. Send your Wicked Game. Send slicing yourself on the cheekbones of a young Christopher Walken. Send Cronenberg. Send your Clive Barker: Patron Saint of Sex Scenes. Send your It-was-always-you-Helen. Send your repressed Ellen Barkin melting in the Bayou. Send your Neon Demons. Send the unearthly pallor of Nic Roeg Bowie, send your Jareth. Send your longing Blanche Dubois, do not send Stanley. No, send Stanley. Send drinking the blood of Gary Oldman. Send Liv Tyler in Tuscan fields. Send Rachel Weisz across the decades. Send Carmina Burana, Saint-Saens Danse Macabre. Send In The Hall of the Mountain King. Send watching the dance through a knothole in the wall to the sweeping sounds of Morricone. Send your American Werewolf, send your James Spader werewolf. Send your James Spader consensual secretarial liaison. Send your Dangerous Liaisons and your Uma Thurman writing desk. Send Drew Barrymore's Cellar Door. Send your illustration of Death, winking. Send your ever-following yellow-clad ghosts. Send youth. Send Suspiriorum dancing lead in Volk. Send Steerpike. Send Travolta before the surgery. Send your Badalamenti-soundtracked Laura Palmer wrapped in plastic. Send your Audrey and the cherry stalk, your Lara Flynn Boyle on a motorcycle at night. Send Mickey Rourke before the surgery. Send hope. Send your Chinatowns. Send Pfeiffer in Scarface. Send Davis and classic, tortured, Langelaan Goldblum. Send Davis and Pitt.

Send beauty. Send beauty. Send beauty.
Send! Send! Send!
Send an ending.

TL; DR: Depressed. Send vampire gifs.

Villain (xv)

So the little girl in the video
was a shock of cold water to me
a feeling of sadness, maybe shame,
not because of any neuroatypicality
— if indeed there was any —
not because of difference:
the difference which must be terrible,
awful, because it is different.
But because it stopped.

Can't remember when I last
leapt   across a room!
sharks on the carpet!
on hearing good news
the not waving
not drowning
but living in my hands.

A gate is shut up tight.
There is a padlock,
a key is misplaced,
or swallowed.
Iron rusts. The story
used to end here.

My Clinic

To the person who said my writing was cold and clinical: A univocalism in I, meaning that the only vowel in this poem is I

This Clinic isn't NHS fit this Clinic is rich with trying.
This Clinic will stitch split skin:
trims stitch by stitch,
skims lightly with timing,
brings light in thin strips,
sings in Cmin, kindly.
My Clinic is Irish,
Irish 'I's smiling, lifts spindly digits,
dips milky digit tips in ink,
writing with inky mind.
My Clinic visits, bringing in drinks, giggling fizz,
fixing things firmly with bird chirps,
with light chinks in misty dim.

This Clinic is misfit.
Smiling brightly, is brimming,
spills in giddy spins.
Kinship with misfit minds—it clicks!
—is rich with impish giggling.
My Clinic is high kicking,
swimming, swinging limbs,
climbing high limbs, slipping,
picking grit bit by bit.
Is King!
This Clinic is mimic, instinct.
That is safer, isn't it?
Bright Miss is critic, brisk snitch bringing dim blight.
Dividing illicit kissing, shining minds.
Thick fists sting, blitzing.

This blinding hit; my Clinic is flinching.
This prickly indignity; my Clinic is crying.

Bright Miss will limit this clinic! It is trick;
criticism is slim pickings; stinks;
will mix this clinic's mind dizzy.
This Clinic is shy, sinking ship;
spits in bright, shining pink strings;
limps in winding rhythm.
My clinic is in bits, stims, wishing,
giving sky-birdish sighs.

This Clinic isn't liking Bright Miss's criticism.
Criticism isn't fixing.
It is brick in chin,
it is flinging stinking vim,
it is limiting living.
Is... Miss Thing stiff with fright?
Wishing ill winds in this clinic:
gifting sly digs,
slick circling.
Sits in wings,
sinning, grinning, winning.

This Clinic, with timing, rightly skips it.
This criticism?
Snip it thinly!
This Clinic will miss criticism,
will miss Bright Miss,
will miss this prickly snitch.
Still it is right. This is it.
Finish it!

This Clinic sits in bright, witch skin;
this Clinic shining.
My clinic is vivid;
is fitting prisms in minds,
bringing sight in blind minds,
is flying with wings in mystic.
My Clinic grins, rising, climbing Birch limbs.
My Clinic is King!
Bring my Clinic tiny birds.
My Clinic sits, singing.
With spirit, this misfit fits in infinity.

Villain (xvi)

But the video still circulates on the internet.
This little girl is blind and cannot see
but touches deeply broken me.
Her fingers reach for the guitar
so she can feel the music but before she does,
touches my lips and asks why I ceased to speak?
Why do I no longer dance her dance,
the prettiest of dances?
Why fold my arms and suppress
the Busby Berkeley in me?
I could only say to win approval.
Her head cocks to one side, asks,
This approval, did you get it?
My slack-jawed drooling bullface
under her fingertips is her answer
and she raises arms,
places hands on a thrumming guitar and shrugs.
Well then, *she says.* Well then.

                                              Dance.

NOTES

Cuckoo references the "brick wall" quote from the film *Village of the Damned* (1960), based on John Wyndham's book *The Midwich Cuckoos* (1957).

Classic Movie Night uses the plot and a single quote "Oh Jesus Christ, no!" from *The Wicker Man* (1973).

The Rape of Solitaire explores misogyny in Bond films, using Solitaire from *Live and Let Die* as an example.

The title of **The Hose, Again** is taken from Buffalo Bill's line "It rubs the lotion on its skin or else it gets the hose again," from *Silence of the Lambs* (1991).

"Her famous blue raincoat," in **Cockroach** is taken from Leonard Cohen's song 'Famous Blue Raincoat'.

The Francis Dollarhyde mentioned in **Butterfly** is the killer in the film *Manhunter* (1986), the first cinematic outing of the character Hannibal Lecter, created by Thomas Harris. The quote "Do you see?" is also from *Manhunter*.

Today, I thought of Eyam contains the line "When we were 12 years old in school, we read of Eyam" which refers to the book *A Parcel of Patterns* (1983) by Jill Paton Walsh. The hymn *Jerusalem* is often sang at the opening of Women's Institute meanings and is considered to be a symbol of hope during times of national crisis. I have used some of Blake's lyrics as inspiration for the NHS section of this poem.

Swan/Suddenly/Suzanne uses a quote from Roald Dahl's *The Twits* (1980).

To Elizabeth, Crying Uncontrollably in the Next Stall is after Kim Addonizio's 'To the Woman Crying Uncontrollably in the Next Stall' from her collection *Now We're Getting Somewhere* (2021).

Villain (xv) contains the lines "not waving, not drowning" which is a reference to Stevie Smith's poem 'Not Waving but Drowning'.

ACKNOWLEDGEMENTS

Versions of some of these poems have appeared in: *Banshee, Anti-Heroin Chic, Under the Radar, Abridged, Room Magazine, Brave Voices Magazine, Eunoia Review*.

When Vladimir Nabokov was interviewed by *The Paris Review* he was asked if there were any contemporary writers he followed 'with great pleasure'. He replied 'There are several such writers, but I shall not name them. Anonymous pleasure hurts nobody'. And I find myself agreeing with this. Maybe I want to enjoy a book privately sometimes, and to write about everyone who ever influenced me would partly take too long, and partly be pointless. Some of these writers are not poets, some of these writers are dead, some of these writers are living poets but will never read this.

But I do believe in giving thanks, especially for concrete things. Some of my friends read earlier versions of this manuscript and told me to keep going. To Tom S. Juniper, Vron McIntyre, Kathryn O'Driscoll and Rebecca Cooney who all reacted positively enough to the poems that I didn't discard the idea, thank you. To the Arts Council of Northern Ireland for not batting an eyelid when I said I wanted to write a spoken word show about survival called 'Cockroach' and a year later saying I wanted to turn it into a book, thank you for giving me money and 'time to write' as well as funding to hire Jen Campbell to help me with manuscript editing and Tina Sederholm who gave me advice on the show script version. Jen and Tina, thank you for helping me to believe that I had produced a cohesive piece of work. That it was 'real'. Thanks also to the University of Atypical who have funded me over the years with a new computer and workstation (amongst other things) where I wrote the majority of this book.

A thank you to Stuart at Verve for shortlisting me the first time I applied which gave me the confidence to submit the (new, improved, longer) manuscript the following year.

I get caught up sometimes in the 'page versus stage' debate so to approach primarily 'page' people for endorsements felt brave for me. I'm still not sure where page ends and stage begins. I'm sure some of you (think you) do know. That's all right. Don't tell me. I'm not sure it matters. So this is to Luke Kennard and Jessica Traynor for reacting entirely normally (and indeed positively!) when I asked if they would like to read a work-in-progress version of the manuscript and provide a quote on it and for being very gracious when I wittered some sort of 'I'm not sure where it fits in the overarching zeitgeist! Some of it rhymes!' comment.

To my cover artist, Joni Marie Augustine who absolutely didn't bat an eyelid when I said I wanted the Cockroach to have a human ribcage and who went above and beyond in services to Being Goth.

To Fay Roberts, who facilitated a quiet writing space every Sunday afternoon since March 2020 with the regular Allographic Write-Ins, without which I likely never would have written some of the more complex (and bloodthirsty) poems in this book. *Larvae* specifically was drawn from the triolet form which was introduced to me in those Zoom spaces and *Three Fictional Women* had been floating around in my brain for a long time pre-pandemic but I never seemed to have the time and energy to write it. To the pandemic... No.

To Colin Dardis and Geraldine O'Kane who kept encouraging me and welcoming me month after month to Purely Poetry in Belfast with my poems that didn't necessarily fit in with everyone else's... and again, it didn't matter.

ABOUT VERVE POETRY PRESS

Verve Poetry Press is a quite new and already award-winning press that focused initially on meeting a local need in Birmingham - a need for the vibrant poetry scene here in Brum to find a way to present itself to the poetry world via publication. Co-founded by Stuart Bartholomew and Amerah Saleh, it now publishes poets from all corners of the UK - poets that speak to the city's varied and energetic qualities and will contribute to its many poetic stories.

Added to this is a colourful pamphlet series, many featuring poets who have performed at our sister festival - and a poetry show series which captures the magic of longer poetry performance pieces by festival alumni such as Polarbear, Matt Abbott and Imogen Stirling.

The press has been voted Most Innovative Publisher at the Saboteur Awards, and has won the Publisher's Award for Poetry Pamphlets at the Michael Marks Awards.

Like the festival, we strive to think about poetry in inclusive ways and embrace the multiplicity of approaches towards this glorious art.

www.vervepoetrypress.com
@VervePoetryPres
mail@vervepoetrypress.com